AF251595

BACKTRACK

And other Poems

John J Powers

London 2005

Front cover art by Mark Andresen

The spelling herein is both American English and British (UK) English, reflecting my own journey. I've chosen to retain any differences.

First published by Dog Ear Publishing
4010 W. 86th Street, Ste H
Indianapolis, IN 46268
www.dogearpublishing.net

ISBN: 1-59858-045-0
Library of Congress Control Number: 2005932689

This book is printed on acid-free paper.

Printed in the United States of America

The poems in this collection represent, for the most part, my experience with Acquired Immune Deficiency Syndrome---AIDS---both on a personal level and as response to the illness and death among so many friends, lovers, and others. I have learned unexpectedly that AIDS is not the end of my life; cocktails of effective drugs, replete with some of the familiar, disagreeable side-effects, keep me quite alive. I am as encouraged to live on as I feel deadened by the memory of this lasting plague.

The shadow of AIDS lingers, of course. We must not forget those who have died as well as the lethal character of this syndrome, even as some lives are prolonged. But I hope these poems express a look toward a future less uncertain and not so necessarily defined in the context of the grim reality of disease processes.

I dedicate these poems to the memory of Noel Carroll, Frank Telese, Simon Kennett, John Connolly, and many others; and to my brother Michael, and my mother, Marie McGovern, d. 2002.

A FALSE DOOR

**A false door was the term used for a symbolic "exit" doorway placed on one side of ancient Egyptian tombs. When the entrance was sealed, so was this door, but it was constructed to provide the dead with a way into the afterlife.*

1.
out from the other side of AIDS
you're alive again
but sometimes
you just want to get it over with
for no reason, not depression,
even anxiety; this feeling
 like losing balance, unable to walk—thinking,
what would falling mean now?

the room is silent except for echoes
of city noises you're hearing
or imagining, not the city
of your dreams, the one living
behind the curtains, always waiting.
something like sorrow but it is not—
like love but it is not love.
cells recuperate in an atmosphere
 of friendly chemicals.

2.
the quality of mercy
is a deception, so you're thinking
at 7 in the morning in a hotel room
in cairo, streets outside
dustier and harder than centuries,
the sand never stops
encroaching, bleeding into
gutters, balconies, a present

 of upheaval, egypt running down.
ghosts chilled in the fever
of millennium. this is a false door,
its frame and aspect
what you think you can
walk through, anytime.

ALICE'S PAINTINGS (REVISED)

alice's paintings weren't originals: they were cheap copies on some sort of cardboard but extravagantly framed and placed everywhere in the apartment, in every room, and every one of them scared the shit out of me.

in my father's bedroom, hiding a growing crack in the old tenement wall, christ knelt at gethsemane, on hard green stones in the black night. his white, sweating face turned upward to his heavenly father. he had long hair, green eyes and wore a magnificent purple robe falling about him. the painter showed off his talent for intricate detail in the flow of the robe beyond the body—the robe entirely covering the little mound he knelt upon. all these years i've assumed he was kneeling but all you see is the flowing robe. his hands were tightly folded beneath his chin. a glowing halo surrounded his head. i don't know if i'm imagining this but i seem to remember an assortment of cherubim in the dark, on high, as it were.

in alice's own room there was a large painting of two blood-red sacred hearts. they were identical in size and set in a bright-blue, solid background. both of them were perfectly unnatural but their vivid colour and odd shadowing suggested something very alive. a very english crown, also identical, sat on top each of them. a large sword cut into one of the hearts from beneath its crown, straight down to its lower tip. bright drops of blood dripped from its edge toward the bottom of the painting. this sword was said to represent christ's sacrifice: i don't know how i know this, but it was distinct from the sword piercing the other heart at an angle, from the left side. this other heart was said to represent his mother, another sacrifice of sorts. her sword went straight through as well, its tip protruding from the heart on its other side, and there were just as many drops of blood. i counted the drops of blood from each heart: there were four from each of them.

in the living room there was a print of a fairly well-known painting of mary in another flowing robe, haloed, with porcelain-white skin, blue eyes, and a transparent veil. an unconvincing hand, oversized for its body and rather plump, came out from under her robe and pointed to the center of her chest, where breasts were politely implied. now i'm thinking that she was a rather italian or even IRISH mary. her fingers pointed to a small heart centred below her neck. the heart was not unlike the hearts above but i think it was blue rather than red. no drops of blood dripped onto mary's light and somehow unreal robe. far smaller than the other paintings, this one was carefully placed atop a library shelf where alice, my grandmother, had preserved very old books from the old country and, for some reason, the autobiography of the american film actress, mary astor, who appeared as the sluttish femme fatale in the 1941 version of THE MALTESE FALCON. i remember how mary astor's eyes filled with tears—real tears—when she realised that humphrey bogart was going to give her up to the police. she didn't express any emotion until this moment, when she knew she was doomed.

NIGHT OF FIRE

(for Jonathan Huxley)

i am letting silence in
even underneath my skin
waiting for sounds
of cars and birds
to inform these words or
helpless night to end

in a soft wind and
slow light of dawn
with the usual commotion
in this street
 workers, children,
 mothers and lovers,
the sun rests
for an extra hour as
summer slows and rushes away

the moon disappears.
the shadow of my head
falls on the page and
moves with me, the full trees
outside my window are
motionless, stunned by
the peculiar heat, and
just now a rush of lorries
in the main road reminds me of—

freeways traveling
discovering
vistas and new cities
hotel rooms with bright bulbs
exposed and peeling walls

drunk embraces,
 aroused and
delirious debate in stupour
of a fading night of fire:

back now
to my own body,
 sensations of fabric and
loneliness, the paling
horizon, animal stirrings
in black and white alleys
outside my door, a digital
clock's unearthly numbers,
one more night lost to itself!

July, 1994
Revised 8/97-2/05

AUDUBON AVENUE

(for my father)

the glow works. when he says, "my son forgot his scissors,"
he's being honest. there are no more trees on the street
named after the famous bird watcher. his step is perfectly
unsure, pure: a white boy. irish. he watches his mother
guide shopping bags in an arc, heavy with shadow, to the
building. terrible black: her clothes and skin covered in par-
lor dust. there are hotels outside: there are no hotels. the
bar, a pinch—tossing on waves, the same, the same, alcohol
and panic, all shoulders, tyrannical—get up the stairs! the
mystery of a living room; here he looks out to the 1950
family car, a maroon, marooned tank; to the crumbling pub-
lic school. he came from HIM. the dinner plates stand on
angles in windows, radish-coloured roses, the shame of
enamel paint—white on everything! clutching a long, light
cane in the hallway, he wipes his sweat from the brim of his
canvas hat.

a new lock makes the door heavy and tight. eight empty
pink rooms flooded in god and mary and sudden, winking
accomplices, damn hillbillies—a hundred pairs of stylish
hosiery packed in one drawer. where did she go? the tele-
phone is like a safe, brick and impossible metal arches cover
the alleyway like wings—she is in the bathroom, washing out
the tub with a lye solution, keeps the door shut so none of
the children can even peek much less get in.... he's like a
kitten scratching at the door frame...his fingers turn color:

the nun who's been waiting so patiently comes back. yes, i
understand, and no one is blaming anyone. you have the
wrong impression. he's more nervous that the little boy on
his knee who sighs and spits on his pants. he touches the

boy's face and smiles, hugs. you're always starving, you're always in a hurry, you always have to get somewhere, do this, do that, like you're a big shot. wait til i get up and out of here. in the silver light, one thin line, he sees her dress—wet, stained with soap, and her face as she turns—a thick mask. you know i would never leave you. you know i'm not doing this to show off. you know it's more than that: his fingers are hot and they shake.

Revised
March, 1999

MISSING LIZA MINNELLI

weird to imagine all wrong with night fires ablaze near federal monuments in deadened city parks thumbs out/turnpike changing to me myself wrong again as i could never grasp being so terribly young what did that mean, young? less so much less NOW seeming matter of flamboyance shouting through blueblack light-childhood of beatings unnumbered humiliations into los angeles *part one scene one* rotting hotel room roaches and rusted keys, miracle outside finally **gay liberation** or, guise of hippie possible dealer pulling me into new world brighter than anything id seen YOU KNOW WHAT YOU WANT said he:alan lowering awesome lank frame onto virginal myself cumming next to immediately then become my own fighting vague would be whitened by amphetamine other theatrics too/hustling boulevards preaching too of l-o-v-e hate ending and revolution terrifying my father rushing into bathroom to slam his fists into my brain for good unmanaging i was there still *scene two* transsexual idyllic among creative southerners one reincarnation and a beastly queen with grandiose silences and gestures to his credit/slide to *part two*, only one scene, new york state correctional for spraypainting churches learning lessons too easily put off in solitary and missing liza Minnelli*

**I had been incarcerated in Spring,1973, the year Liza Minnelli won her Oscar for 'Cabaret'. None of those in solitary were allowed to view the ceremony.*

BACKTRACK

(for Chris LaCava)

wake up, he says, licking his lips on the microphone, the
sound of a mauled serengeti wildebeast chasing them out of
the unheated room; whiskey nurturing his self-righteous
demeanor he hurls a catalog of abuse into poor thin air sav-
ing himself, the table of contents, sickness, lying, creeping
age, exotic disease, fucking god, habits of dreams, glossary
of so many undeadening desires, furniture quietly replaced,
that pounding, somebody's weak hands clenching, laughing,
burroughs made it to the end, no surprise, hitler got there
before him let's see now, i have two pairs of solipsisms, the
dealer grimaces revealing the trinity, three of a kind,
embarassing the rest of the ensemble—let's give them their
money back, their two cents! roars rumbling back to black-
ened plains as the old timer leaps to the podium shuffling his
notes, coughing, before i go on i'd like to say—oh get on
with it! the national park, the casino, some undigested
material for tacky performance, legs wobbling, vision dou-
bling by the angry second, i wish i had a river, witnesses
nodding disapproval, not enough, you have to admit we're
dazzled by routines! that pounding: rifleshots, flames,
armies of birds racing against the sun, the plastic faces
erupting, kings searching for lice under each other's crowns,
queens rescuing former apostles, twelve singled out, concur-
rence among entrails: assorted narrative diversions—did you
know me when i was hungry? tapping, is this working?
somebody get harry up here from the basement, if your
mother doesn't know how to get here you can always...chill
of unarguable emptiness, always departing, throngs, silences
white and wide as the moon, one tear.

clearing his throat he shouted after all there is something to
be said for *divine pain*! his first impression wasn't far off the

mark, this solution should be manufactured and distributed with the appropriate disclaimer or at least a warning.

he gathers his composure—get those animals OUT OF HERE! a cadre of surly well- endowed security guards usher the wounded into makeshift...temples, the pounding resuming: one more crack and i'll make gambling *illegal*! some girl from pomona squealing what affrontery: her grandma hollers fire! fire! we've come to the end, let's search him! (pause) open his legs wide, wider, that's it, you can just make it out— THERE! but your honour that's impossible, even if you estab- lish motivation he couldn't possibly have kept a flask up his asshole for what is it—*seven* years? you're confusing the issue. look at that. is it necessary to be so...the courtroom, the national park, the casino, what else...look at his library. unable to provide an alibi appealing for mercy, oh my god. you'll admit extenuating....

the glibless proprietor allows the feeding schedules to be entered as evidence, exhibits a thru z, just enough to avoid complications/keeping the jury out with formulas, death threats, movie deals: it's the holiday season and i'm sure we'd all like to get this over and done with so we can go home to our families. someone mentions the investors, pen- sioners and other halfwits conned into buying shares in a dubious venture, a business park with day care facilities in the negev.

his body collapses, his head hitting the microphone. mum- bles into white sheets: not both ways, you can't gamble *and* pray with the same conviction, naturally you're likely to mis- take a collection plate for a bill of lading, or a summons for an invitation to a one- time-only benefit for...part-time work- ers, refugees spending hours sorting donations from a last- but-one garage sale.

"i don't know where you think this line of questioning is getting you," so pronounces her honour; one of the jurors writing in his notebook his understanding: everything in quotes
is forbidden, seeing the light between curtains he fondly
remembers daytime television, missing so many episodes
because this queer was preoccupying the court with—

drowning, if you close your eyes and relax you can swallow
the whole thing without as much as a...sigh, the wrong
word. i have the place surrounded! call headquarters and
tell them...no, wait, they won't listen to you unless they hear
my voice.

the liberal bouncer swore on a stack of bibles, the wellmeaning naturalist actually suggested we might hear from
another source—the wildebeast! but it wasn't a feasible
option since the season had been such a disaster anyway
and how can one possibly expect to make any money and
retain the GOOD WILL of all concerned unless you keep the
casinos open twenty four hours; this rubs ecclesiastical
authorities "the wrong way." we're entirely forgetting the
repayment owed to the millions deprived of their land so you
guys could do your orgasmic rituals with slot machines and
chalices...

wait a minute, hold on, something seems to be...yes, i can
make it out, it's afternoon, i'm in a northern climate and it's
winter so it gets dark very early...been up a couple of nights
and i keep worrying, not paranoid, mind you! but if you are
unconvinced allow me to backtrack....

TESTAMENT

i like this song, he said,
rolling his eyes (this wasn't a night
i was remembering—this is not
a night i remember)—he paused,
agitated and alone,
as we all drank ourselves into
stupors of fragile enlightenment: incredibly
resonant clarities soon
forgotten (none of this is true)
i warn you, i'm going to get up from this table.
(i was impressed: your eyes moved along
the cracked ceiling) yet it's impossible
to imagine that evening without him
(it is impossible to imagine that evening)
he walks to the toilet, a hard smile
hiding something (i don't want to remember);
the toilet's as private as a coffin (disagreeing,
pulling me aside, stop romanticising!).
my trousers stuck to my ass, i'd been
so incontinent i couldn't pull them down (these
are not years: i lasted a few months.
the infection got so bad i couldn't walk——)
all right, he tells me to stop it now,
behave (these are not tears)—
the less melodic, the less comforting songs
are best left unsung—certainly i won't write
one with you! the trail of such enveloping
misery, he remembers—
would you have me sacrificed like the god
you would reject...crucified to accommodate
the need to be released...
you shall be released.

1997-2005

ENOUGH SHADOWS

for Noel Carroll

(after Allen Ginsberg's HOWL for Carl Solomon)

I saw the bodies of my generation become pure shadow,
coughing, burning, wasted,   crawling in desolate alleys
wanting love or an anonymous fuck,
Who with misery and wet sheets and sedation barely open
eyes hoping for another   body to stifle commotions of
mechanical monitors, private screaming,
Who open skulls to release clutters of dementia vibration,
Who fuck and suck like it's going out of style and it never
does,
Who pray in newly painted hospice cells, words collapsing
under purrs of omni-
          present television,
Who preoccupy themselves with empty moments for their
own sake,
Who get used to stool samples and x-rays and tentative
smiles,
          mothers rehearsing funerals with no malice intended,
Who know they're destined to canes and catheters and per-
petual retching,
Who explain their shame in terms of impregnable sorrow,
Who drift into queues of moviehouses thinking they're wait-
ing on line for lab results
          surrounding this infection, that side-effect, unwaking
fully alert in piss-doused pyjamas,
Who habitually accumulate quandaries like wandering jews,
Who laugh at graffiti reminding queers not to forget their
last breath
          when they get fucked up the ass,
Who awkwardly come to meaning now meaning has import
since nothing else is so
          unworldly,

Who avoid ingratiating sympathies, vague acquaintances
now thrilled to know him,
Who discuss god as if god had not created—like everything
else—the cruel joke,
        irreversible rites of passage parodied into therapy ses-
sions to appreciate
        "what AIDS has done for me,"
Who are tempted by salvation, drawn out of a hat of flowers
and lies,
Who loses trousers in claustrophobic chaos of backroom des-
peration or joy,
        panicking, revealing islands of lesions on cheeks once
coveted by the best of
        them—who is the best of them! Proud sodomite
especially now, delighted
        to participate in romantic *fin de siecle* delusion of ulti-
mate demise,
Who's in a room locked in a body resembling a jigsaw with
pieces moving and
        disappearing before even a hint of his own human
form,
Who is not recognised by someone he knew before the
plague now excited enough
        to want to make babies, 'til she's embarassed to recall
his face, now
        shell-fish thin, bones comically propped up to mimic
my forgotten man,
Who is not brave enough for bouts of bloodletting and pain
obscured by morphine
        and gushing consolation,
Who secretly begins to distrust proven ideas, his own body,
a circular earth and
        distant sun
And who wonders whether we should have left the firma-
ment, we should have settled for unknowing so our bodies
could lie still,

Who is arrested and raped, with fingers crossed, he might
come to his senses
        after all,
Who would be surprised to hear his withering god's wither-
ing denials and
        know he's talking to himself,
Who hears they're burning books again and offers up Celine
dancing on Jew graves,
        Dickens and Hugo for making poverty romantic,
        and reluctantly Artaud, sensing his words wouldn't
take to the fire,
Who fakes his signature on credit applications so he might
know Istanbul before   departing,
Who tries to keep the noise down moaning as familiar jolts
of pain return because
        a student nurse forgets his schedule, and
Who won't forgive you, your children or their children for
        rationalising many a last moment,
Who cannot bear to embrace anyone, cementing traditions
of abuse, dysfunction,
        sacramental guilt, exotic suffering,
Who is in this room, lying on a low bed trying to sleep and
        who keeps coming out with—
Who admits he should have known evil inherent in penises
and blood,
        listens to latest rumours, marketable hopes for sur-
vivors,
        wondrous cures, dream, insults to dead friends and
relatives,
Who sometimes is enchanted by amphetamine because it
gives off the stench of death
        and suspends hours and tears before they come,
Who doesn't like the stench of death but prefers it to the
odour of affliction,
Who likes to think he is alive and thinks he is alive and is,
        bowing to no one with a voice, to silences and all
shadows,

Who should have known enough to keep their hearts
attuned and minds alert—
     And who begs the night to end, and taunts the new
day with his own shadow,
     before the light will say *enough!*

San Francisco, London, 1997-2005

THE FALSE GOD
for Don Mark

the false god talks to me. he understands
my lack of faith but is unforgiving. he
appreciates my self-doubt, says i can
re-interpret it positively, 'be humble.'
'look at it this way: i know you have
created me,' he says, 'but that's no
excuse.' thunder rumbling over the london
skyline, dense pellets escaping the
firmament. scatterings of tourists,
soaked, undeterred, stream into
the british museum. 'excuse for what?'
the false god giggles; i avoid his shadow
in the crowd, but his voice—my voice—
embarasses everyone. people who just
a moment ago showed they could
weather...any weather...blush in his
sight: their eyes meet. 'something else,
isn't it?' 'you would know me now if you'd
make the effort! if you would have made
the effort,' in the clearing, riding at
eighty miles per hour on a morning express
train to cambridge.

London, England, c.1995

CAMOUFLAGE

the dozens of lesions
have turned his face
into a nasty pattern
of purple islands
in a sea of regret
with eyes, nose and
mouth obscured,
humbled in the extreme,
but the comedy of make-up
and flesh-coloured cream
gives drag a new profundity:
he can be happy, painted
like a '50s queen at
twenty-two, holding court
this time around
to ward off loneliness and
death—really nothing new.

San Francisco, 1994
Revised London, 1997

CARRIER

love's beyond me
never
minding sheets, stains,
the mess in my mind,
it was tuesday morning:
your body climbed up
my stairs, tentative with
every step, meeting
my still-death gaze
as you reach my door—

pleasant green, secrets
relayed in gestures,
smiling barrenly—
knowing this is
a clasped moment
neither of us will let grow,
loneliness unappetizing
food for thought, much
less touching:

you won't allow a kiss
as you unzip your jeans,
an embrace out-of-the—
words, stream of neglect,
polite as tea,
say something, reading
under, not between, your words:
"let's get on with it."

"think i should tell you
i'm *positive*"—you're drunk
and horny enough to react
like so what, with a smirk,

rubbing your crotch
like a gypsy, this is your crystal ball,
the future is getting your rocks off.   *Revised 2005*

DISTRESSING AS KIERKEGAARD
(a la Babel)

His smile opens like a doorway. I make conversation (look for something to keep the door from closing), but he affects adolescent awkwardness. A Cool distance of politeness, harsh as winter breezes, rushes in. We become a bad movie either of us could walk out of at a moment's notice. We do meaningless camera movements around each other's bodies, noticing shoes, talking shoes, talking styles, about as distracting as street signs (new ones with no words which I suspect are designed to deny obedience to a vengeful god a la babel), slide our way through a-r-t, collapse in a desert of -isms, finally crash into theories, religion, politics, black humour, flaunt our own attitudes like highway cops, degenerate into absolute truths like perilously sexy uniforms and myriad fabric, striped trousers distressing as any Kierkegaard anecdote ...nervously hoping all the time something would bring us down to earth when suddenly

A pause, pregnant as a fish, drops its fragile eggs in our laps; we become mothers to this idea, adjust our dicks casually enough to stop beating around the bush, stop pushing away each other's nudging legs. A storm ensues, a friend named Rebecca appears to know him, promises to pull him off the road, onto the shoulder for A BITE TO EAT!

Curving into digressions on national cuisines...we nearly collide discussing Hitler and the vegetarian psyche. At last, I have to get off this runway, and when I do I notice the beam of his smile, squint and sigh as my vision returns and I notice the glow of *other* lights.

March, 1997-Revised July, 1997

FIN DE SIECLE

a moment, literal in my mind,
undone by reverie, blind
faith in treachery, bombs,
routines of banality,

playing at history:
articles of faith derided,
lovers, like victims,
brutally misguided

as media take over,
every dream's won over
really and virtually;
ending the century.

London
May, 1999

VEINS

(In memory of Simon Kennett)

*Then I went back into the house and wrote, It is midnight. The rain
is beating on the windows. It was not midnight. It was not rain-
ing. (end of MOLLOY by Samuel Beckett)*

i wanted this nurse to collapse in shame—a blue and dark
shame so permeating and long
she'd never live it down, so to speak—

i was waiting for an IV to be administered—a long tube with
a bag of antibiotic or some
such thing at one end, ending on the other side with a metal
and plastic syringe plunged
into your arm—

into my arm, i mean: fuck the royal WE...i hardly can
breathe as i write this, the liquid
jolts, the liquid erupts in my arm (the liquid does not
erupt)—

pain: burning, simple fire, body wrapped up in one point
and moment. looked down and
saw that the IV liquid was pouring into my muscle, creating
a little lump: the liquid
creates a little lump, i'm shouting for a nurse. i did shout
for a nurse, i was shouting:

she's there insisting. she'd found a vein and i was overreact-
ing—the patient, the mere
patient, fucking the mere patient. "where did you get your
training, in Auschwitz?"—and
she was out the door.

someone eventually really found a vein. my poor little veins,
like yours, like the royal
WE, try to be accommodating. sometimes we collapse
under the strain. other times we're
still-blue and deep and listless...

December, 1998-Revised 2005
London UK

FIRST DAY

i thought my lease on life
was up but here i am,
the first day of spring,

 this mirror
lies but i'll believe
 anything
now; give me your hand.
guess this means
we're in love.
let's walk to the river,

watch barges and skips
move out of time, with their
own destinies, rippling,
disappearing,
black water
nearness; in his image
i find myself
 unraveling
my body,
swim free.

London
March, 2001/March, 2005

FORTY-FIVE

i keep thinking, what a wilderness. it's like when i was young—i must have known it then, these perfect white hills under a black sky of raining stars—i came to this place and said nothing: in those days i'd never ask the popular questions revolving around "where do i fit in?" i knew better, for better or worse. knowledge is somebody's sick joke, i don't like those apples. the number forty-five shouts at me: quaint syllables turn me into a hieroglyph, my body flattened and turned to one side, i wonder if you can only look in this direction, you can only think like this: jesus, you were provided the luxury of an early death, demise—i keep wondering. what happens is natural enough: when you are eight years old it takes so long to get through one day. at twelve the day's already dense with possibilities and urgencies: at sixteen everything is important and you discover truths and barriers and lies. words and dreams comingle, the structure of a leaf suggests something beyond metaphor. imagine weariness setting in at that age, the victory of weariness, as if you know something. at 23 you're drowning in alcohol and drugs and romances, insisting nothing's fleeting as boys and passions not to mention convictions lose their charm. these were my quick years, stumbling over each other, then i noticed i was thirty, thirty years old. i thought i would shiver at the thought beyond the flip of a page on my personal calender. i fell asleep in front of the television. suddenly awkwardly i was in my thirties: look at those boys, no longer among them: imagine turning vile, separation breeds contempt—and a new embarassed love, in my thirties i was embarassed more than anything. not yet nabokovian but close: unexpectedly, the wilderness opened up.   i saw the forest AND the trees, the strongest wind couldn't knock me down, not this girl. i was young again. young at thirty-seven may not be the same as—never mind. there is a luxury in forgetfulness. meanwhile the television became a

phantom: over the years the image got more and more con-
vincing, so much so i began to question my own dimensions.
it's no good saying wait a minute, these are just images in
an electric box in a corner of the room—who would believe
you? they seem indestructible, and seeming...seeming is
everything...the structure of a leaf is undeniable...but i keep
wondering.

London
August, 1999

GERTRUDE'S PROBLEM

(for Paula)

from strength to strength
to weakness, to weakness: maria callas,
eyes rolling,
bassey-like intensity:
this is a poem by a queer—
is this a poem? a poem
is a rose in every room,
gift of nature parading in the clothes
of an open dream,
what's an open dream?
this was gertrude's problem:
dazzled, a bit shaky
as picasso kept insisting, don't move,
while hamlet blamed her
for everything—
crawling out of the studio,
patronizing polonius, ezra pound:
burning synagogues, from strength
to madness: barbra streisand,
bellowing, i can't help thinking
i'd have been better off a drag queen,
bitterly alcoholic, lip-synching
"oh my man i love him so."
meanwhile, gertrude had to make sense of
her son's agitation:
the prince of denmark finally
resurrected the wounded mothers
of guernica, something is rotten
in the state of—
i can't go on. what were you doing
with that sword? good lord.
not two minutes ago you were

a good boy; the heir
to the throne—then you turned
every woman's head at avignon,
pablo, and one night—this is the future—
maria will make her comeback at
covent garden, trying to forget
aristotle, which is besides the point.

London
May, 1999

SOME STARS

barely above a hot chimney
in a thin line on a hill
with a rolling fog

my teeth and eyes move—
chatter and blink
before a slight vision.

o loneliness is so long—
i didn't mean to use the word.
some stars suddenly appear

in colours i've never seen,
frosted in a light blue distance
where they are traveling alone,

detached and glorious,
posing a natural threat
to my silence and delirium.

some stars are a matter of love.
they shed no light without a sigh
calling over years to come—

to come to rest in the arms
of a fantastic image,
the body of god in chilled night,

barely above a hot chimney
in a thin line on a hill
with a rolling fog.

JOHN J POWERS
Atlanta, 1979

NOT JUST YET

my body is crawling
 toward the millennium
it says "feed me!"
 hamburgers, roast pork fried rice,
 chicken in a basket,
french fries called something else
in this country...
it says "hold me!"
 perfect strangers, even regretful
 lovers, my mother's tentative
embraces held longer,
 longer each time,
it says "heal me!"
 cocktails of euphemisms,
 aimed, firing at poor little things,
 viruses, exotic or erotic cancers,
routine infections multiplied so
routine becomes obscene!
my body touches the hem
of the millenium,
down on my knees, she frowns,
winks at me as if to say
not just yet

LARGER THAN LIFE

everyone lives one less day than they deserve. She would have walked her dog in the new neighbourhood. He would have smiled suddenly. He would have visited his mother in the new development. She would have apologised, then regretted the gesture since she had done nothing to offend her lover. He would have sung a song from his early childhood in the shower, keeping his voice soft. He would have hated himself with almost suicidal vehemence. He would have learned how to line dance to give his mother a thrill when at last she would have visited him. She would have sighed. The boy would have burned his uniform. The tourist would have figured out a bus schedule. Jonathan would have liked the song they're playing. Noel would have rolled his eyes and felt ashamed and amused. Simon would have terrified everyone around him (force of habit). Elizabeth would have not missed the next episode of Eastenders. Richard would have continued to regret everything after a style. The popular dancer would have lived out her life, her entire life, in Nuremberg. He would have rented a tent in the afternoon and drove for hours to catch the sunset near 29 Palms. She would have finished the easy questions drifting into a twilight slumber. She would have lost 7 children in a head-on collision with a drunk sailor who would have missed the last bus back to the base. He would have invented a new word. She would have considered homeopathic remedies and yawning exercises. He would have worried about his ongoing problem with coordination. They would have rooted for the opposing team. The ministers would have guaranteed the prevalence of famine in the country which once had been their territory. Marie would have had the odd sensation of burning her finger when she touched the TV screen. Total strangers would have robbed a popular old woman on the estate—robbed her of everything, all she would have had left to her name, and they would have laughed over her collapsed body. He would have changed his tune. She would have written to the local council about all the whores on Sycamore Street. He would have picked his nose and blushed. The baby would have realised a syllable in a split-second, a moment she could almost grasp with her fingers, larger than life. The engineers would have torn the blueprint into tiny pieces and dropped them into the steaming furnace.   Vivian would have finished her plans for her daughter's birthday party. My lover would have hesitantly reminded me of his disinterest in monogamy. James would have lit a cigarette, and John, at this real precipice of his energies dissolving....

GASPARA STAMPA

(Mark Andresen)

gaspara smiling. for you she is not veiled
in the past, a woman with strong bones,
tall, simple and elegant in dress,
with dark, long braids of auburn hair,
at a wide, high window in a sparsely decorated room:
she writes on heavy parchment with a long feathered quilt,
foreign rhymes and familiar rhythms,
—a lover
she remembers so clearly she does not
succumb to grieving, his body is present;

gaspara frowning, then close to tears:
he waits, sensing a subtle possibility,
the centuries are not like doors!
breathing, she turns
and becomes another kind of artist, living not
far away, not possibly forgotten,
their bodies the same, untainted
by linear myths of years, geographical gaps—
she lives in a suburb of new orleans,
tossing flowers into lake la freniere.

London, 1999—Revised 2005

SHADOWS

these are the shadows
these are the shadows we have to live with
these are the shadows we have to live with
who have to live with other shadows
these are the shadows we have to live with
who have to live with other shadows
dancing like children
these are the shadows we have to live with
who have to live with other shadows
dancing like children on broken glass
these are the shadows we have to live with
who have to live with other shadows
dancing like children on broken glass
pretending
these are the shadows we have to live with
who have to live with other shadows
dancing like children on broken glass
pretending otherwise—

Revised December, 1996
London, England

FUCKING AIDS

this fucking illness. first minute it's there, then there's the next; i mean the next minute, hypochondria, fall back to waiting, fucking waiting, home from hospitals, back from the clinic again, the AIDS clinic, the fucking AIDS clinic. fucking AIDS. fucking logic of uncertainty, look at this way, you might be hit by a car, we're all going to die; this said to cheer you up, put things in perspective: fucking perspective! so everybody's waiting, everybody imagines they're going to die in a couple of days *or maybe not*. fuck, maybe not. everybody looks at their skin and panics. everybody thinks the world's come to an end when they get something like a cold, the common cold, the fucking common cold. fuck this shit, wait a minute. most people don't look at their skin and panic. most people don't think the world's come to an end when they...there's logic for you. i keep coming to an end, a way of trying to be reasonable, fucking reasonable. anecdotal banalities floating in my head, out of my head, out of hospice wards and...out of my fucking head. someone's bound to note i'm feeling sorry for myself, my fucking self. my fucking self brought me here, to where i am, mistaking doublebeds for comfortable coffins, one comfortable coffin, what a word: dying is NOT an art, the way i look at things i'm supposed to be alive and preoccupied with other things, other bullshit instead of stalking the grave. fucking AIDS is a hard business, a girl doesn't know where to aim, how far to go, how far to go before...uselessness, like death itself, unlike dying. oh but there *are* so many other diseases...TB or not to be. humour's not so much a remedy as it is a kind of detour, eyes and mind averting the gallery of bodies just behind this jeweled curtain—i'm beside myself, i've gotten to know these eyes, this smile, years marked by transience and keeping up with...keeping on, going on, fucking going on. sorrow is a luxury, the real privilege is murder, bloody murder: knifing the bastard in the back, before he sees my face, before he can threaten me again, before he looks at me again with his straight face, his defiantly straight face, and he says calm down. he tells me i am a survivor but i'm exhausted and really ungrateful to this partner of mine, this partner with the scabs and the skeletal grin and the hacking cough, the fucking hacking cough. but he's quite willing to accept all this lunacy as part of something bigger—something like a syndrome of sins, like fucking AIDS. .

London
October 1997

GETHSEMANE

(for LM)

knowing this is no coincidence—
the commotion of metal and stomping
 feet, the way they are, even at a distance—
and those lazy boys passed out,
i imagine them as my own children:
huddled under trees, wrapped in wool
protecting them from this strange
 cold wind.
anyone would laugh at me
with my swelled eyes, awake for days
as if there were no such thing as light,
and andrew telling me to stop
moaning and acting so afraid—
like something was about to happen,
knowing this is no coincidence—
they're closer now, so close
some of the boys are waking up,
wiping sleep from their eyes,
i love them like this when they're
aroused and baffled, but the noise
has become deafening. soon enough
someone will ask, god,
 who am i?
i keep wondering, creating a story
in my own mind: metal and wood,
death and—what is that voice i hear?
the darkness is the same, but one
of the boys has come over and
held me in his arms, whispers
 nothing to fear:
you have your whole life ahead of you,
so we share a smile and yes,

i will do what you want:
metal and wood, death and—
"new life," he says, touching my face:
a child's smile, a feminine body,
and, at the approach of these guards
with their military demeanors, he is
the one who offers a kiss, soft, held,
  and lasting tears.

London - August, 1999

GINGER

my life as a canary was uncomplex
and unfettered, you might say:
i must have started out smaller
than i was at the end—probably
a lot smaller, like a little yellow pebble,
 except things stuck out
and they became little feet and eyes
and a less than impressive beak,
but why should a canary have an impressive beak?
domesticated, i was a genetic homebody,
if you opened my cage
i wouldn't have known what to do.
you might think i'd have wanted to leave,
but that's a superstition—
for years now the domesticated canary
has been quite content sitting on a wooden perch,
jumping down to the bottom of the cage
to shit, or flying, if you can call it flying,
up to the water and food boxes to nibble
and slurp:

just after the woman used to feed me
and pour the tap water into the box,
she'd watch me eat and drink and
swore she saw a little grin on my face,
and she'd say to her company—who were a rare group
of women who looked exactly like her,
"ginger's happy today."
but she could not take my death
any more than i could. One day
i was dozing, on the perch,
and felt something like a belch
and fell over. the last thing my little eyes

saw was a vague definition of stars
beyond the drapes in the living room.

London
September, 1999

NO WONDER

her fingers and toes
are almost webbed,
creating a suspicion
among the faithful;

her lips quiver
and eyes seem to shift
at the same time,
a bad sign;

her father's profile
isn't visible
but it's coming,
and somehow, unknowing,

unraveling mysteries
without waiting, worrying
or disbelieving,

her fingers and toes
clutch and stretch;
eyes, lips open
and breathe, bearing smile,
removed from legacies
and learning,

alert as a bee
among flowers, others
alarmed by the sting
of her unformed, uninformed grace;

'til she becomes
something of a daughter,

tangible, lost to accumulations,
certainties, no wonder!

London
Revised 2005

POEM FOR KARLA FAYE TUCKER
(executed in Texas, 1998)

i don't know this woman
but can imagine.
i can imagine she wouldn't
give me the time of day.
she'd smile and pity me
because i'm a fairy or maybe
she's virulently anti-homo
i don't know.
she lives in a prison.
she needs a better hairdresser.
her husband seems to have her
wrapped around his finger.
i've always objected
to that religion she espouses,
that happy blood sacrifice!
anyway she's from a small town
in texas and i hate even the idea
of small towns in texas. hearing
this she'd be furious,
she'd want to get back at me
and all i represent
all she imagines i represent
or all i imagine she imagines
i represent, whatever,
but she should not die.

February 3, 1998

LAZARUS THE QUEEN

1.

shed no light. if you move you'll create a shadow,
stop it now,
his father's voice—do you imagine you're different?
THEN the tyrannical embrace,
i'll tell you the story of the witch in the mountain.
the witch who lives in the cave in the mountain.
if a breeze comes up from the sea
she freezes in panic: restore me to stone and wood.
now, now—take care of those tears!
his father burns a cigarette into his tiny arm,
hovers over him, mingling tobacco breath, love,
words, you thought it was going to be easy.
he would make no assumptions
from that blue morning, allowing daddy to decide
everything, like leviticus—born in a golden book.

2.

i don't like these clothes,
i wasn't born in them,
i have no knowledge of these hills,
the red landscape, the boiling ocean,
where i am, becoming, frail and simply
frightened, frightening, everybody looks at me
with knowing stares—avoiding eye contact
all the time, his shadow dwindles,
he is the pride of the demon
with his belt and candy, alcoholic silences,
makeshift memories, silly conceits—holy father,
i am proud and bleak, i will not survive!
when he talks like this
daddy knows what must be done. saint rose

of lima waits on a misty street corner,
limp and yet overbearing, offering
holy communion. her genitalia is stainless
silver and bloodless, deadened
over nights of violent caress—

3.

the story ends. saint rose went back
to needlepoint and fire,
his father began to recognise
his own shortness of breath,
the sky closing in; by now the boy
discovered other shadows, still
avoiding eyes and the awesome moment
of touching, skin, hair, a multitude of
glowing bodies finally made out in the dark—
different with a capital D,
look at the world they offer me.
rose was dead for centuries, daddy
was on his way, mirroring corpses
with his clammy, green complexion.
hospital-green, death-pale, daddy's shadow
fell away, and the boy came out to play.

4.

the queen is in her element.
the queen's able to laugh heartily
and long, her dress replaces
her father's tacky nightshirt,
the one he wore straight into his coffin
uncomplaining, never complaining,
while she secretly assembled
her queer entourage, joking with them,
affecting holiness for their sake—

then one day he fell in love.
his eyes and broad, infectious smile
lift HER away from himself and
familiar rooms;
two score and seven years
ago she was blown, for the first time,
but though it felt like a curse, the old sin,
he did not freeze, unlike the old woman.

follow this story: in royal splendour, denim,
leather, with romantic ballads ringing
in her ears— "once i had a sweetheart
and now i have none"—he collapsed
in OTHER arms, dethroned at last!

5.

the story does not end!
a grey-yellow plague swept over the land.
noel, john, jonathan, frank, anthony,
charlie, ishmael, loren, richard,
simon, and so on, vanished on separate
mornings—at least they were separate mornings—
until it was his turn, or so he thought.

but now, now our queen rises from the grave;
his doctor calls him
one of his "resurrection boys."
phrases like SQUARE ONE
keep coming up, embarassing
and absurd...always square one, another one:
just yesterday he noticed how the slightest
trace of cloud over a full moon
can suggest a halo, and how the circle glows
and slowly grows until the night is filled with light.

London
August, 1998

LET IT GO

you're full of yourself, she says,
trying to change the subject—
"i will remember everything
and i will remember everything
again, and everything will be the same."

trying not to think.
a dialogue comes from somewhere,
she's impatient and
knows when i'm trying to impress
rather than—

streetlights outside my window
keep me up at night;
television, of all things,
mocks everyone
in its path—how can i sit still
with all these moving images?

"forget them," forgetting them,
"forget ever knowing much less
believing in them!"
your own living room lit up
by patches of colours, drowned out
by rhythms of bombs, commercials,
commentary, drama, anecdotes...

when did i come into this room?
i can't make out a thing,
the light's fading, here's what
i was hoping in the dark.

the electric light made us comfortable
but it took away the night—"but no,"

she whispers, "it cannot
take away the night!"

i will remember everything
and i will remember everything
again, and everything will be the same.
"everything is the same."

London
September, 1998

LIFER

he's asking himself questions
like he's never asked them before.
london's an unfamiliar shadow
falling over his face.
the bronx is old, dirty,
unforgotten but still a mystery—
los angeles gleams, san francisco
is one lonesome street too many.
this new orleans drag queen
with the shiniest eyes tried to
steal his wallet. in echo, utah,
he got stuck in long silence,
hours waiting for a ride, and hours,
and in prison he met a lifer
who introduced him to marx
and even lacan, even lacan!
his mother was a casualty
before he was born
so he will never show her this—
daddy's crisp and not even
rotting anymore: EMBARASSED
roots seep out of his grave,
he still REMINDS them how to behave...
and his brother is a facsimile,
perfect to his unquiet death,
soon enough.
atlanta crawls
into view, drag and drugs,
and can you believe he
joined the fucking navy?
when he was eighteen
he knew anna, an old drunk
who slept at the gates of the white house,
had nowhere else to go so joined

the vigil against a war, and that war
still goes on.

stuck in a small farm town at
the border of indiana and ohio,
where the time zone changes:
unable to get a ride, for eighteen
hours...there is a motel there
which is one hour different
from one side of its walls
to the next—they like pretending
it's meaningful and tourists are
thrilled to be in one time and the next
at the same...
taking pictures of clocks,
how the hell do you get out of here?
how do i get out?
if i'm lucky i'll get a ride
through pennsylvania, toward new york,
in one shot, and he won't ask me
to talk about what i do, or maybe
blow him in shadow light:
detoured to florida, what am i
supposed to do? monotonies of
memories too personal...
but i remember, and the lifer
was young when i knew him,
when i really got an education
and he is still there.

London
February, 2000
(Remembering 80s)

COMMOTION

the gleam of moon
confused in lamplight, someone reminds me
of the cliche, the glow. i get excited.
youth's wasted on the old.

the precious needs to be relaxed.
silence needs to be endured
like a commotion, exactly
like a commotion.

London
March, 2001

NOT DEAD

(in memory of Allen Ginsberg)

imagine dying in our new wars,
videoized: green or grey uniforms
hiding bodies lost at carthage,
waterloo, stalingrad, resurrected
with new money—

hurrying to boot camps
to avoid prison or the street,
hopped up on voices
from a new wilderness—TV;
fucked up with new lies,
wonders—stealth bombers for
the air force, cool designs for
sleek tanks for the infantry—

everything so new, so now:
a new cause for the new world:
a paradise of malls everywhere
and the holy marketplace,
the faithful queuing up, into
the new cathedrals of capital, multiplex
cinemas, where anyone is projected
pretty, buffed, enthused,
exciteable, even dead
though not really.

London
April, 1999

MOTHER: A Portrait

(for my brother, Michael P.)

(1)

Think of her as a girl during that war
Huddled behind a window shade
Listening to Sinatra, rumours like troops roaming streets of
the Bronx, who would have thought?
Time passes, does not. Eagerness in dreams.
There will be a man with a pure smile.
The streets filled with bulging, curved, expensive
Automobiles. He's straight out of a b-movie,
polite out of nervousness:
I will take you places you've never seen
And truth to tell, she would never see them.
Her father warned her about smooth talk but she's thrilled,
now: eyes and a smile take her to dinner.
Cigarettes. He doesn't mind that I smoke, of course how
could he? He's like a chimney himself.
We're from the same neighbourhood, both Irish,
In the Golden age, we might as well imagine
Ourselves. John Garfield, Lana, promises. The GI bill, I tell
you before long we will have our own house in the suburbs,
she's nodding. Something
Uncertain stands watch between them, she imagines slaps,
hollering, endless night: someone will have to look at this,
at a distance, maybe the boy rumbling
In my belly, at least I think it is a boy.

(2)

Could be a girl. Sinatra's broken into the movies,
How could you think of that lanky body without a song?
Even tabloids start spreading the news,

Not just of silly marriages and movie deals
But Freud, analysis! The wrong air, shouting, paralysis, guilt,
god, baby-boy bands. The world's ending or maybe not. I
may have a multiple personality, you never know. Look at
Joanne Woodward.

She's thinking like she is expected to be thinking in the asy-
lum, the madhouse: God has a lot of nerve, but only whis-
pering, here because I did something wrong. Everyone's
here because they did something wrong, why else? Hints of
Christmas. It's December, a kind of December. I came here
in February, nearly a year ago: at least I could figure that
out. Help me.

Do you know what day it is? Do you know where you are?
Who is the President of the United States? Where did you
live before you came here?

The word "here" is like a nudge. Marlon Brando was married
to Teresa Wright, I remember that much, and he had a terri-
ble war injury and she was trying to be supportive but he
was...bitter. You have to get rid of that bitterness: Teresa
Wright is perfect though neurotic. I'm 24 though it's funny I
never tell anybody my age, I mean not that I'm looking older
than...do you think I look old? It doesn't matter. Do you
have a cigarette? Funny when you think not so long ago,
the idea of a woman smoking would be... *I guess looked
down upon.* I'm glad to be leaving, I mean as soon as I can
be leaving, it's up to you, I guess.   I don't know, the other
girls tell me I should say as little as possible. You start ram-
bling and they know you're not ready.

(3)
the Bronx is some sort of heaviness, the streets fuck. Out of
the blue I'm sent to recuperate. This is the first but not the
last time in my life I encounter Lucille Ball, on television.

Thirty years later I will be watching re-runs but they will seem so fresh. I can't help laughing though any exertion makes me wince: you have to watch that. The nurses say if you even see a hint of a grimace, or a wince, you should administer morphine. EVERYBODY comes back, the room is so crowded, was I hallucinating mornings? Taking out the garbage, feeding the dogs? After a while you realise the light here is very different. New York's light always seemed distant, like nature itself. Los Angeles interferes——the impression of nature is...I should let him say it. He would never ask me what I think, this is what regret is for, he says to himself now, now, now. On the outside you're vaguely instructed on how you can pull yourself together. As the last gate opens, the first man whom I'd ever met in hospital, Abe something, carries my bag and says, "This is the age of chivalry." I think, what are you trying to do to me?

(4)

music's new, lots of drums, craziness. Frank Sinatra is rumoured to be about to marry Ava Gardner. We've moved to a new building across the river in the Bronx. Someone upstairs has a colour television! The colours are bold and unreal, how they get them to come out of a little box in a room...I mean, I don't know. It isn't like the movies.

Who would have thought? Today I have a hundred chan-nels. I can just lie here and click through countless visions even without commercials.

Coming back. Here she is propped up in a coffin, she never wore so much make-up, not even as a bobby-soxer. What would it be like, seeing yourself, like this—still-silent engulfed in chemicals, perfume, suffocating flowers: this is where I am now, near celebrities forever, a panic of movement and memory held, sealed like a photograph: a laminated body,

decaying in los angeles. The old building in the Bronx is for-
tified with steel and cameras, you can call the police at any
time, all hours, from the lobby. You've forgotten your keys,
a weird stranger waits in the tiny entranceway with a hot
grin. A fire blazes from the roof downward, all the neigh-
bours you never knew parade into the courtyard, with blan-
kets and animals. I have my old copy of Sinatra's *Only the
Lonely,* a collector's item. Nobody talks to me except for a
woman named Rita, who talks to everyone, in the elevator,
on the street, and at home to herself: she's on the ground
floor so you hear her all the time when you're coming in.
She speaks as if she has to remind herself where she is all
the time. You're home now, you're about to make dinner,
you have to go to the supermarket for garlic, and so on.
The voice is vivid and clear. She is next to her door now,
waiting for the alarm to stop. "It's almost always false," she
says. I'm thinking now I don't have to worry, I haven't seen
Rita in years, she probably wouldn't even know who I am—
—

Los Angeles
January 10, 2002

NEVER ENOUGH

one body is never enough, that's why ants
race into formation
under the sole of my shoe,
patterning themselves after
the very shape of my right foot,
looking up, not one of them complaining,
dancing and dying, crackle of a thousand
bodies, a dachau delirium,
meanwhile down the street
she is twisting his arm, telling him
to get into the closet, keep quiet,
what is he complaining about?
in the darkness he feels content,
he abandons being alive,
opts for lasting silence,
drawing the moment out in black,
his only defense! you have to understand.
the funeral parlor near his house,
named after an irish immigrant
long since dead, has never known
such business—even the war
was less lucrative
than this unending peace
in the face of—
multitudes, commotions in alleyways,
occasional speeding trams,
matches, hurricanes, cholesterol,
cutlery, cutleries, pharmaceutical
shortages, ongoing market trends,
laughter in rooms—never enough!
she waits for her last meal. there's
even a priest and soft music,
a quiet walk past all the others,

their eyes shut in bizarre reverence
for someone who just has to go—

London 1998

NOTHING NEAR TEARS

(A poem for Matthew Shephard, killed in a small town in
Wyoming in October, 1998)

i don't imagine your body
for no reason: on television
you're an attractive blur.
it isn't enough.
i don't think of your slim body
for no reason: i could fall in love.
i could have fallen in love.
i can't fall in love
with you now since you're plainly dead.
let me hear your voice.
not last words, not begging your killers
to let you go, nothing near tears.
on the night you were murdered
what i imagine is that i met you
and led you safely away
to a motel room. in the dark
we held each other: instead of
torture and mutilation and finally
death, you're smiling:
instead of being pistol-whipped
into unconsciousness in
the name of god,
you're masturbating, your eyes
closed, hands moving along
my own body. you come easily.
we look for a towel.
the prairie night outside is alive
with stars and coyotes howl over
the hills just beyond
where you picked me up.
i leave before dawn, regretting

not saying goodbye, as you hurry
into your clothes to get to class.

London, 1998

78   John J. Powers

not saying goodbye, as you hurry
into your clothes to get to class.

London, 1998

OMNISCIENT TEARS

bring us into this room. bring us to the bed and tell us to take off all our clothes. bring us to an awkward silence: he leaves for a moment to get something he forgot...we're sitting naked on a stained mattress, unable to say anything: knowing the routine we know we're expected to be silent, even our breathing is measured. we're already crying—omniscient tears. the routine is so familiar we don't have to wait for the belt, the wheezing sound of leather—pauses so dramatic they will inform our lives forever, accentuating the ritual: we are not worthy to receive you: the blows fall hard and quick, telling us, after all, we ARE worthy. nevertheless we jump about the bed trying to escape each blow—we compete, each of us narrowly avoiding the next blow, or feeling it: feeling it. speak but the word and our souls shall be healed. wordless constant unstoppable blows: two young boys with bodies, wracked with pain, their father doing what he has to do. bring us to a place beyond HIS exhaustion—he does not stop until his breathing is so heavy he has to take a time out, regretably: my father hardly can breathe, his heart's in such a state we feel sorry for him. we feel sorry for him. on occasion he will appreciate our sympathy. get dressed, he says: we're less relieved than annoyed; after all, he didn't go as far as he could—he did not beat us to death. we're resigned to putting our clothes back on and acting as if—what? as if we'd failed him somehow, but he instinctively knows how to deal with our guilt. he offers ice cream and cinema, milkshakes and JASON AND THE ARGONAUTS.

London
November, 1998

THE OTHER AIR

1)

speaking for the black night
          empty of images a night of lonely rooms
                    secret
children who do not know the past
          only harmed to think of the future
                    and quiet time
          in a real world
outside prison—
the prison of embraces and burns,
hellfire and chocolate,
          songs and leather equipment:

silences and romance, hurried
          conversation, fashion, newsreels,
perfection;
          electricity, phrasing, when i was young,
          always tomorrow, roads, fantasies, the thrill
          of a disease;
                    non-stop waking, mirrors and
mornings, god again;
purity of television, the way of a sentence,
          violation, reverse word-fuck,
                    fun digressions, timidities of verbs,
                    helpless, passive, nothing here
                    (what did it mean at one time
to speak aloud
in an open field, an echoing
voice heard through villages...not possible
          to merely imagine, trapped
in a prison of twentieth century, Anno Domini) OLDER
                    now
          at the moment laughing at himself

                    only right
                              he discovers
the brevity of *years*
& likes to think at 39 he can contemplate the universe

"speaking for the black night"—
a naive victorian invades his consciousness—
something's all wrong:

2)

molds and visions
hypnosis of pop music rhythms
daily grind
reports on wars, celebrities, architecture,
breathing in
a glimpse of folding memory—
questioning poetry
academic questions in a dead friend's
eyes and words
what are you doing
what do you want to convey
how do you confront your own
        spiritual laziness; he liked
        the word spiritual,
imagining a god who had His problems, always had.

i wrote him a letter
reminding him
how doomed we are
in the context of beards, false prophets, mankind,
sedation, human sacrifice, jesus!

he knew the arguments, died
in a stranglehold of wondrous faith—
(in his heaven,
he feels sorry for me)

3)

but since
but since
i can't think of anything
or a world without him
i'm always outside, hearing vibrations of
ecstasy, songs for dancing—
angelic beats, soft, continuous:

then i realize where i am,
a gay bar in New Orleans.

but since
but since
i'm touched with something
so dramatic
it's fatal
i'm outside the world

looking outside
looking in

my body a true host
welcoming the end

only if
only if
i will breathe
for the first time
the other air.

(San Francisco-London)

PATIENT

 business of waiting
getting too close,
this withering of my heart
too real, words drag
inside, outside my mind, like
canular, catheter, anti-retroviral,
skeletal, begging, snoring in
too many beds, blue nurses
and worn issues of magazines
nobody reads in day rooms,
mock libraries of forgotten
detective stories and romances,
overcooked meals reminding
every patient, and patient?
what does that mean?
a friend visits and muses
on the word, how did it come
to represent these people?
this business of patience,
stalling like blindness,
dreaming of one day, week, month,
year more, and so tired, tiring.
encroaching self-pity and
a style of guilt: i could have fucked
him before—what am i saying?
he has a lot to answer for,
down from his heaven, blue eyes
gazing onto this page, muddled
thoughts, broken in pieces
like a body, unworthy: like
it never has made much sense
anyway, being—

London
April, 2000

PLATO'S BABY

One: The Polite Blood

you cursed your knees
violent
ly sinking, the L-shape somehow
sudden
ly fair, the baby of Plato. fingers,
warm, close eyes, mother
promising, or promising
the man, coy as a virgin, waiting
for the polite blood:
                         you is, you is.

handle the spoon correctly
as if you can
conjugate, imagine. now
          the sun is a vibrating moon.

                    look at him!
                    they giggle
                              turn
                    dry up like land

LOOK AT HIM

september...november...
slap-happy he's able to confuse
blinking with permanent loss of vision,
the dear boy dazzles...infuriates
father's heroes,
then, like a devoted slug, finds his way into the garden

Two: The Boy in the Temple

rhetoric like elastic
bounces off walls in the holy rooms

spoiled, startled
everything around him revolves, blurs,
disintegrates in argument disguises charms
fervor, reconciliation
                    a lost hope, a heedless design

and mother's here (sorry) - she brushes into

Him, smiles;
twin beams warm the classic faces—
only men, only hurting
                              realising frailty in numbers
                                    words racing
'til they topple each other
                    for one pure view
                              learning the art!

Three: The Wedding at Cana
     "hello, I'm Jesus, and I'm an alcoholic."
                    a hush felt like a hurricane
                    loud inside before suddenly
                              this is it!
                                    teletype rattles out of
                                    a future
                                    rips apart the famous tab-
ernacle

                              breaking in crevices
                              collecting
                              draining out
                              predicting
                              the valleys of California
                              tentative cover stories
                              booze, children, faith
                              whispering forever
                              local wine!

THE bodies relay

a look gesture
a thumb
an eye and a big frown, centuries betrayed
or these years
after all these years
moments
after all this—HE COMES!

> it's enough to make
> a healthy girl on the coast
> fall to quick ruin Irish-style,

> DT-ing eternity.

Four: Lazarus

wildfire.
creased, false costumes jump out of
stone, sealed boxes where
the pure history of families lies, rises in dust,
music of a tale, stirring,
yes, i know, of course, naturally, by all means,
without a doubt:

> (a knowing grin gets Him started.
>   He has to remind me,
>   don't you know who I am?
>   i want muscles, sweat,
>   a soft gleam, un-
>   certain eyes)

yes, i know, of course, naturally, by all means,
without a doubt
> however

> STAND BACK
> push pull
> breathe in
> out repeat

                              wait. out in
                              feel for a pulse
                              tell me you don't get
                                       the idea
you don't believe!

                        (he's weak, He's tired.
                        they kiss. when they're
                        finally alone, their chests
                        touching, lips held,
                        he understands.)

Five: Song of the South

it's not that
it's not that
it isn't that we don't
it isn't that we don't
it is not that we do not
it is not that we do not appreciate
it is not that we do not appreciate

we have our responsibilities
we do have our responsibilities
we do have our own responsibilities
we really do have our own responsibilities

to the people
to the people
to all the people
to all the people

chosen, chosen. and we're overworked.
and we are overworked.
and we are overworked.

it's not that
it's not that
it isn't that we don't

it is not that we do not
it isn't we don't see but YOU have to see

                you have to see
            there is only one jehovah.
            only one.
                one, father of dreams.

Six: Part of a Dream

you're perfect, you undress, you lie down.
you hold up your arms, turn your head. you're
trusting, unafraid of awkwardness,
the pounding, relentless commotion in my head,
filter of years, an assortment of melting,
softening, colourless candles, coins, and tears.

what could be wrong?

the minute i saw your enamel eyes i knew.
the minute i heard your hollow yet high voice i knew.
the minute i touched the plaster curves,
hard torso, the funny curls of impossible gold,
the smooth thin lips in front of a mystery,
a wire, and a bulb, and the polished, absurd neck,
i knew.

Seven: The Last Supper

the corner of the child's eye
peeking   baffled, curious   only pretending
as metal wood food words circulate

the plate and frame vanish
the yellow light slowly fades

voices converge

in the shadow-glow of dying flames
unknown faces
a busy, heavy ritual, legs, grunts, sighs,
soft denials, hands
and the shadows of trees make him jump

       the possible:
as he approaches the familiar body
his fantasies submerged in a quick all-knowing glance

he's propelled like a mosquito into the dry
           maroon night

Eight: The Passion

anything but this
anything but this pain

this body
convenience, memory—beyond me

       a body doesn't believe!
       i could forget everything!

   flesh
    rapture
   loving, surviving

they tend
to overlook you anyway
all the effort

character, sense memory, an umbrella opening,
    breaking to pieces,
    with only the narrow stick left—
    a cane. mother's breasts, full, swelled,
    waiting. a table. we haven't got all day,
her cigarette smoke lifts.

she shuffles in her seat. i know, Jesus,
i know how hard it is; she rolls her eyes,
her face reddens, the music from another
room stops, she stares at me, jerks her arms
high in the air
    to wiggle into a burgundy sweater.

"the heavens fall," she mutters,
pinching my face. her stunning language
    your decipherable
conceit—MY GOD! I AM WORTHY!

this body isn't a vessel,
temple or vacancy—
blood, bones, flesh, celebrate,

the heart beats, the rhythm endures,
so I am not yours,
Father—or anyone's.

Nine: The Mystery of Faith

(You come from me.
Your body is a figment of my imagination.)

when I am with you
for an atomic time
alone close to light
aroused in the privacy of our embrace

solemn narrow pure—I lose my breath
                    I lose count
              I lose sight of this mission
these souls   your response
              the sense of this death
                    this one time

the death of fathers mothers sons daughters colour symmetry
              spiders edges memory memorizing behaving
                    talk tenses rhythm
death of knowledge beauty stupidity words reaching lips

        water wheels the death of swords similes
              touching waking up necessity
                    silence shoes pain longing & love

(You know now.   Now you know.)

San Francisco, 1988
Revised in London, 1998-1999

POEM (for Ronald Tavel)

gets hairy sometimes
falling into this pose
where i say something
everybody knows
or such false modesty
as can be seen in the glittering surface
of the bay in moonlight
false because it's so sincere
waves lapping concrete, unassuming light
of streetlamps and bodies surrounding
black space arriving—
falling among these idols,
who pretends to be unpretending,
she's younger than she knows only
her body betrays a violent betrayal.
i forgot how to say what i was saying

you get your appetites
by crawling and denying, i'm always
finding myself looking somewhere else
to somebody else, where has he gone?
what happened?
the drifting tide slows over hours,
morning interferes and I'd get excited
because the bars will open.

London
February, 2001

REGRET

his first smile
in the black room
when i was ugly
frowning in a window
 of rain and
cold
 overdoing one
hug so important
it has to last no matter—

  a kind of begging
inevitably, the indulgence of
pretending we're untouchable
while he's riding among stars—
i mean now; or maybe
in empty silences, awkward,
 penetrating,
below a moon and floating, dreams;
he forgets! we are
the strangers we never were
always: the room brightens
with cold morning,
bar advertisements gleam
menace and pain,
 the exact science of loneliness,
talking, time passing,
what was i thinking?

London
March, 2001

ROMANCING ADDICTION

these are my last words beginning again/about how i've lost
friends/waiting for a fragrant smile diplomatic and eager with
narrow and quick conversation with a dimly idealised dealer
of my old drug of choice/a tainted variation of amphetamine
sulphate itself unmysterious hardly even enjoyable in the cool
sense only what will happen/i come close to dissolving
becoming true blue phantasm unnoticing a racing heartbeat
this body ending unending noticing mind consciously stum-
bling over unwords meaning filtering away ideas hurled
up/into the air of smoky clubs to meet devastated strangers
flaunting anonymity forgetting silent commotions/fears/empti-
ness years and persistent loneliness in a foreign city/crying
and trying to remain remembering dream domains innocence
breathing-in/not unwords countless and colliding among men
apparently with better things to do naturally enough/not to
listen to rampant enthusiasms at delirium-edges as a mock
holiness sets in/reeling and always waiting until ALWAYS dis-
appears/poor night no longer boasts the burden of darkness
and cool air/sweating and cigarettes take over/images ride
high outside failures of dreams or even silly death so a mild
psychosis akin to hope and wondrous redemption/deception
for once able to shatter morning/again able to lie creatively
about freedom become unawkwardly unknowing "how" much
less WHY/returning to earth to routines like hearty meals edi-
fying cinema or ancient thrills logic or passions except this
one lasting several blank hours in something like time unsolid
impure near-deadly/poor night at last intruding in the dis-
guise of SUNRISE and traffic where only now he is begging a
page for lack of release until one more and ONE more excit-
ingly ominous fix before um sleeping

London, 1994
Revised 1998

untitled (for Rrose Selavy)

roses know how to behave
in the wake of merciless night,
hurricane winds, natural flames,
ice, torrents, in shadow;
petals lighter than breezes

May, 1998
London

SEVEN DREAMS

i am in a frozen world
and everything is frozen
and i m-m-mean everything.
still, stillness, not in motion,
not like everybody was caught
at a moment, kept standing,
sitting, sleeping, dreaming like statues:
since memory is f-f-fiction,
even undiscovered, we're happy,
even if happiness never occurred to us,
ha-ha: hints of what is never to come
all over the place, some nut advances
the theory we were once soft and warm
in her own mind since nobody in
this world communicates.

i am with elizabeth taylor in 1965,
after her return from Haiti.
she had filmed graham greene's
THE COMEDIANS with her new husband,
Richard Burton, about the fall of Duvalier, but you wouldn't
know it if you watch the movie: the wardrobe
suggests they'd rather be back in ancient
Rome, where they met: CLEOPATRA and Mark Antony,
pretending to debate history, fucking offscreen.
i tell her she should re-consider playing Martha
in WHO'S AFRAID OF VIRGINIA WOOLF?
she asks why and i explain that, should she play
the role, every queen in the world will want to imitate
her imitating Bette Davis, which is confusing.

i am falling upward, a surprising gravity
pulls me into the deep blue of stars, moons,
classical music—hear the echoing words,

cinema's unimportant, the echo losing
clarity as i shoot past jupiter, uranus.
the mind being so limited i have to imagine
someone is pulling me—how else can
i explain a trajectory defying even light years,
light years so light i wave past with a baby's smile?

i am with my mother in an orange room.
the room's walls are like rubber,
and any time we say anything
we feel dizzy almost to the point of nausea,
as if this orange room is a moving box,
and various hints, foregone conclusions,
come to our minds at the same time:
airplane seats appear under us, holding
our bodies, and we both use the tiny
nausea bags at once: "thank god,"
says my mother, with a howling laugh
that makes the whole room-box turn, and turn,
and the orange turns to a more pleasant beige.
the beige automatically comforts us:
then it turns to an almost fierce, institutional
whiteness, the movement stops, we hug
each other, completely, becoming one.

i am confident, onstage, in an unplayable
play, supremely unperforming,
the crowd anxious but suddenly
beautiful: all astonishing latin males
with roughness and pouting in
t-shirts, with blue tattoos so prevalent
they are the dominant colour in this
theatre, and naked from the waist down.
four of them are masturbating naively,
like no one's paying attention, but
they're right at the point of coming— "oh jesus!"

i'm shouting, and this is received like
a bad joke which does not go down.

i am extinct without knowing it,
cascades, collages, routines of images,
intervene: a holding pattern
allowing anachronisms as attractive
as intimacies, descriptions, certainties
of knowledge, mammal, intellectual:
a daydream, so convincing i almost
forget: bones and flesh, dust and sighs,
like mourning, without—

i drift away from barriers of walls
and sky, "this is no dream,"
confidence belies somnambulance:
freezing again, i see my breath
in this air, telling its own story:
in london, in northern cities, dawn
is late and breaking without ceremony,
 we don't
know if we're awake or we're still
asleep, the sun mocking our alertness—
almost scandinavianly suicidal,
i am saved by cinema!

London - November, 2000

STOPPING

I came alone to this wilderness
and heard a voice asking
what's the dance floor like
which sounded like a joke
but there are no jokes here.

so I said, it's fine
if you like it so loud
you can't hear yourself
think, but why should you
want to hear yourself think?
(embarrassment ensued:
bodies were falling over
each other: i use the past tense
to suggest imagination)
always dreaming,
the privacy of loneliness is *exact,*
like a recipe. the stars fall,
the prism of night offers
consolation, no street is dead
when i'm in this mood, no eyes
betray anything beyond what they see.
and WE ARE NOT COMMODITIES:
the race of pigs and warriors weep.

London
July, 16 2001

THE SCIENCE OF TREES

(for Rrose Selavy)

trees hold up my neighbourhood
like curtains, raised so we feel
we're important, we walk by
ambivalent or pompous,
or stumbling, imagining an embrace,
magic: sighs of these limbs,
coughing stumps, trunks
attached to the sky like swords,
flickering flames, buds, drifting
acquaintances unlike
anything trapped here——

London
July, 1999

UNSLEEP

father forgive me
for the torture of houses,
rooms i'm able to hide in
to escape from you

the scent of attraction
possibilities you pick up
follow straight to me
ask feebly honestly
why i have not taken my vows:

along the way
of this penance
i forgot them
balancing lies, other sins
in your name

i keep thinking in your name

unable to close my eyes
to figure the difference
jesus lover father

bones
masculine
                    affections
          aiming,
weakening—now *we* are the dead,
not Joyce's star and snow covered memories,
we're alive, gleaming,
skin almost brittle,
unable to swallow,
breathing routine—tears flow readily,
a blood stream, windows clouded, air so murky

and weirdly cool yet humid enough for a plaque—
    a drama of dying, undying, unsleep

London, 1998

112   John J. Powers

and weirdly cool yet humid enough for a plaque—
    a drama of dying, undying, unsleep

London, 1998

THESE THINGS

you wouldn't know me now
especially if you're wide awake
anticipating sorrow or shame
and i come to you
with my belt unfastened
and a spookily seductive gaze—
with the remnant of a body
more than a physique, scary enough
for you to look the other way—

germs and viruses get the upper hand
without a joke or an argument.
this is a hospital bed.
the curtains around my area
of the ward do not BREATHE.
demonic snoring keeps me alert.
he is able to lose himself
in REM sleep, the motherfucker.

you wouldn't know me now
especially if you're able to sleep
through the night and i come to you
more shadow than ghost—
eerie enough to remind you
of plague and death—
voiceless in honor of the dead—
breathless in discreet mockery
of everyone able to breathe freely—
humorless and embarassed for it
since humor's supposed to be
a sign of life
going on in spite of these things—

London, 1998

THREE ITEMS

"To them that think
Death's honesty won't fall upon them
Naturally, life sometimes must get lonely."
        Bob Dylan

1. LONELINESS

loneliness is like a blasphemy
you're not supposed to admit to,
a way of saying i am here, alone, period.
consolations, gestures, remarkable language,
sunrises, diligently prepared meals,
tentative or eager embraces, intimations
(these crippling truths, like abrupt changes
in the sky, or complacent laughter
where you are now waiting!

2.

i've come to something
but this is 2001, supposed to be
just another year, like 1954, or 1978,
but why doesn't it sound the same?
and who thinks the year sounds so foreign,
 after all?
just this second i'm hearing
BBC news telling me
new genetic engineering
will change *how we are.*
a moment later i hear
that the bumble bee is disappearing,
and there is panic, somewhere.
"the bumble bee plays a CRUCIAL role."
desperation, media drama.

i was stung on the forehead by a bumble bee
when i was six years old. fever set in.
and i began to worry.

3.

feel like i've been on hold
my entire life—
music in variations
of regret and wistfulness, alternates
with quick silences, ready
repetition, the preoccupied other end,
what's impossible?
somebody's having a good time.

London
May, 2001

TRUTH

the griffith observatory
recognises stars
existing beyond history

 remember natalie wood,
james dean, sal mineo AND
madame dennis hopper.
the truth is black holes
and distances, time bursting:
obscure astronomers plastered,
celebrating ever-new finds,
sal mineo crawled (crawling)
to his death while james dean
seems to register
real shame, goodness:
you might have said
you were staying overnight.
i usually sleep alone,
but how can i not IDENTIFY?
the universe expands, also
collapses (collapsing), curtains
and dreams. sal mineo
went onto b-movie purgatory,
television and christ!

August 24, 2001
London

UNBELIEF

be suspicious of a god who's in a hurry
or even worse, a god what takes its time:
the rush is a lie and patience
never was a virtue. a world of climbing
and weeping, laughing and deciding, or
killing,
is endowed, beyond belief—

London
March, 2001

THE BOXES

I have known your face
For so long it gets spooky
To reminisce with others
In the same room, nostalgia
Embarrasses you,
Like all these stained boxes.
This isn't blood along
Any of the rims (corners?).
Ink or wine is drying.
Rioja from a wedding
Turned quickly deathly,
The fierce, repeated
Underlining of old-time
Instructions, before the plague,
And the lists of things to do,
Flamboyant or vitriolic
Commentary from diaries
Of make-it hundreds
Who can only use red pens
Now, less symbol than
Irresistible, like energy.
The boxes cry, seams moist
With tears, muddled
Testimonials, glycerine
Retreats behind the scenes,
Away from One of Vigo's slow cameras.
The movers never come
When you want them to,
Like the police, deadened
Themselves from rumours as
In who will pay for all this lifting?
Why does the night lend itself
To such horrors? In one
Of the boxes I see your body

Writhing like Poe's joke.
Someone waits outside the door
With an old fashioned, hand-written
Bill of lading whilst I mold myself
Into a corner, squirm.

JJPOWERS
London
March, 2005